From my dear Daughter Sylvia & Son in law F[...]
for my 78th Birthday June 26, 1986.

ALSO BY JUNE SPRIGG

By Shaker Hands
Domestick Beings

INNER LIGHT

INNER LIGHT

THE SHAKER LEGACY

Photographs by Linda Butler

Text by June Sprigg

ALFRED A. KNOPF NEW YORK 1985

THIS IS A BORZOI BOOK
PUBLISHED BY ALFRED A. KNOPF, INC.

Photographs Copyright © 1985 by Linda Butler
Text Copyright © 1985 by June Sprigg

Library of Congress Cataloging in Publication Data
Butler, Linda.
Inner light.
1. Shakers — Pictorial works.   I. Sprigg, June.   II. Title.
BX9771.B9   1985   779'.92898   84-48664
ISBN 0-394-53256-2

Manufactured in the United States of America
First Edition

A Note from the Photographer

It is remarkable that the Shakers, a religious sect that was at its height over a century ago, can still speak so eloquently to the contemporary world. There is something in the vision of these people that stops us—the pace and complexity of our daily lives exist outside their doors, and for a short time there is a respite.

I recognized this on my first visit to Pleasant Hill, Kentucky. The summer morning sun was streaming into the Centre Family Dwelling House. Everywhere I saw light—reflected off the white walls and arched ceilings, pouring through the skylights, seeping through the windows above the doors in the halls. Within a month I was back, chasing that light with my camera, trying to catch it on film. As I worked, I felt a growing reverence for the people who had lived in these spaces.

This body of photographs is my individual response to the objects and buildings that are still with us. I did not attempt to document accurately the present-day Shaker sites, although I went to eight of them. Nor did I try to reconstruct Shaker scenes using only Shaker-made or period objects. My reaction was first and foremost an aesthetic one. Some aspect of an object or architectural space would speak to me, and I would attempt to pull out of it what I saw or felt.

In all but two communities, there are no living Shakers. Yet how strongly these people speak in the things they left behind! The buildings have an undeniably spiritual quality, and, a century and a half after they were built, they show evidence of a clarity of mind and vision. They were designed to evoke the spirit of God, and they do. There is a quietness in these simple lines and stark surroundings that facilitates a focus beyond oneself.

So, too, there is a relentless perfection in many of the Shaker objects. In a cloak, each stitch is exactly in place. The lid of an oval box is neither too loose nor too tight. The fine quality of much of their work suggests that Shakers transcended aching backs, tired eyes, and the inevitable boredom of repetitive tasks. How? They tell us in written records that their work expressed their love of God. As I study the delicate curve of a spiral staircase or the fine handwork in a silk kerchief, I can only conclude that many of these now nameless Shaker craftsmen knew a greater peace of mind than most of us ever attain.

Much has changed in these Shaker spaces since these objects were created, yet much has endured. The spirit of the Shakers lives, apart from how many individual members remain. In the spaces they built and in the objects they made, there is a strong spiritual presence. It hums in the mind quite on its own:

> *Tis the gift to be simple*
> *Tis the gift to be free . . .*

LINDA BUTLER
Pleasant Hill, Kentucky
1984

On Turning Toward the Light

Let me tell you about a place where I like to go to write. It is a room on the third floor of a large brick dwelling house in the center of Hancock Shaker Village in western Massachusetts. The village, a trim assembly of yellow, red, and white frame buildings, is rooted in New England, by the grace of a mile or two. From the window on my right I can see the New York hills that begin the world west of the Yankee realm.

The building is vast, with more than fifty rooms, ninety-five windows, and six stories from cellar to upper attic, but this room is small. Seven steps take me from window to door, five from wall to wall. In the manner of things Shaker, it is simple and functional: plain pine floor, white plaster walls. A pegboard circles the room over my head. Next to the door are a closet and a tall built-in cupboard and case of drawers, butternut and pine stained yellow and orange. The twenty-four-light window is very large in this small space.

At first, all appears perfectly plain. But look more closely. There is care in the proportions. The drawers decrease slightly, pleasingly, in height as they rise. The wall pegs are hand-somely turned, when mere sticks would have satisfied utility. Each peg, threaded at the base, twists easily into or out of the pegboard—much extra work for the carpenter, but an admirable bit of foresight, since a tall cupboard would fit flush against the wall with some of the pegs removed. Like an ellipse, or a chambered nautilus, or three lines of haiku, the room possesses a simplicity that is not lightly achieved.

The room is a fine equation: the sum of wood and plaster, plus light, which endlessly alters the look of this place. Mornings here are dim and blue. Shadows curl like cats in the corners. I want to move softly then, as if the room were still asleep. By noon, if the day is fair, the walls have brightened, become crisp and white as starched linen.

As the earth turns toward late afternoon, something special takes place. The room fills with light until it can hold no more, and in this fullness is transfigured. For this moment and a short while longer, there seems to be more than wood and plaster, line and plane. There is harmony, radiance, and a bittersweet glimpse of something like grace. It happens this way every day as the room turns toward the light. It has happened this way for some fifty thousand days since this room was new in 1831.

I like to think of others who have known this moment in this place, especially the Shaker Sister who first lived here. This was the bedroom, or retiring room, which she shared with one or more other women. Her name, her age, her reasons for being here—these are things I will never know. Still, I feel a kinship with her in the way this room has held us both.

Here she woke in the dim blue dawn, stretching her toes in her narrow bed. Here she splashed cool water on her face at a washstand. She smoothed her hair under a white cap at a looking glass which was hung, I imagine, from one of the pegs near the window to catch the soft light of early morning.

She hung her plain woolen and cotton gowns in the closet and folded her stockings and shifts into the bright orange and yellow drawers.

There was little else in the room: a chair or two, a stand for a candle or lamp, a strip of woven rag carpet, a woodburning stove, the universal small jumble of things in places where people get dressed (combs, odd buttons, a dish for the soap). She owned none of these things, not even the clothes she wore. All was provided by the community, and all belonged to the community. When she needed new stockings or more pins, she asked the Deaconess down the hall.

The dwelling was a hive that buzzed and hummed around her. Nearly one hundred members of her large communal Family shared similar rooms along the hall on this floor and the one below. Sounds carry in these bare plaster and wood halls. She heard talking and laughter, coughing and snoring, and the deeper thrum of Brethren's voices from across the hall. In the mornings when she dressed, she and the others in this room stepped around one another like slow dancers. The scent of coffee floated up the stairs from the kitchen far below. At the signal for breakfast, the Sister and the others filed downstairs to the dining room to eat: wheat bread, butter and jam, fried meat, apple sauce, boiled potatoes.

Like a great heart, the dwelling gave rhythm and life to the village around it. The Family assembled here to eat, dispersed to fields or workshops, gathered again at noon for dinner, dispersed once more to work, and returned here at last when the day's work was done.

When the Sister left this room, where did she go, and what did she do? Spinner, weaver, cook, seamstress, gardener, physician—what was her place in the whir and motion of the Family's industry? When she returned here late in the day, what did she think as she sat in this place and watched the light fill the room? She had heard stories of the hard times, now forty years gone, when the Family slept fourteen in a room, when wheat bread and milk were scarce. Perhaps she herself had lived through those years. When her thoughts turned toward the past, the new home seemed a blessing indeed.

All the world was bright for the Shakers in 1831. With some five thousand members in eighteen communities from Maine to Kentucky, the Shakers were the largest and most successful utopian enterprise in existence. Neat farm villages bespoke their prosperity; the rousing dance worship that gave them their name testified to their spiritual vigor.

The sect's fruition was all the more remarkable in view of its origins almost sixty years earlier. In 1774, a thirty-nine-year-old working-class woman brought eight followers from England to New York in search of a way of life based on the spiritual and material simplicity that Christ had taught. The sacrifice of self-interest for the sake of community was at the center of Ann Lee's vision of a more perfect society. Celibacy and communalism were necessary means to this end, she believed. Ann's proposed heaven on earth was not easily achieved. She was imprisoned, became impoverished. Her husband left her. In five years she did not win a single new believer.

As religious revivalism swept New York and New England, however, Ann and her followers made converts. In 1783 Ann preached in this valley, where her millennial message attracted the interest of several households. By 1784, ten years after her arrival in America, a few communities were beginning to form, and Ann predicted that members would flock in like doves. By the end of that year she was dead, but the sect continued to grow. In 1831, when the Sister first watched the light in this room, the woman Ann Lee was a distant memory, in her grave nearly fifty years. But the vision of Mother Ann had never been stronger.

As membership grew, the search for ways to live in harmony became more important. Although people who joined the Shakers renounced the imperfections of worldly society, they could not leave their own failings behind. Shaker life was not freedom from human contrariness but a profound challenge to it. Conversion was neither a retreat from temptation nor delivery from evil. Instead, members confronted every ordinary smallness of spirit in themselves and in each other.

For Shaker society to succeed, the group's welfare had to assume precedence over individual interests. As the sect grew, a series of practical solutions to the special problems of celibate communal living gradually shaped a distinctive way of life in Shaker communities. Like a clock, a Shaker community worked because many small parts operated together with precision and order.

A typical community had two or three hundred inhabitants, divided into several large communal Families. Families were like neighborhoods, self-contained and within walking distance of one another. A Family consisted of from a few dozen to as many as a hundred members, and had its own dwelling house and workshops. Two Elders and two Eldresses in each Family were in charge of spiritual and behavioral concerns;

Deacons and Deaconesses handled practical domestic affairs. Families represented different orders: a Gathering Order for trial converts, an intermediate Junior Order, and a Senior, or Church, Order, whose members signed a covenant to certify their complete spiritual and economic commitment to the society.

The Families clustered around the Church Family (in some communities called the Centre Family), in whose group of buildings the Meeting House for the entire community stood. In this village, in 1831, when the Church Family moved into its new dwelling house, there were six Families in all, with a combined membership of about two hundred, within a mile of the room where I write. The Families were characteristically named for their relation to the Church Family — East Family, West, North, South, and Second (between the Church and the East).

The Shakers were unusual among celibate religious sects for living in groups that included men, women, and children. Each Family of adult Brethren and Sisters shared a large dwelling house, but the sexes occupied separate quarters, used separate stairs and entrances, and sat on opposite sides of the dining room and meeting room. An invisible fence down the center of the dwelling divided their home into parallel realms. Men and women knew each other by name and by nature, but their lives intersected only in carefully prescribed ways. Small mixed groups gathered regularly in "union meetings" to talk or to sing. Individual Sisters and Brethren were not permitted to meet privately or to pursue feelings beyond the bounds of brotherly and sisterly affection. Children, who were brought into the community with their parents or as charitable wards, lived in girls' and boys' houses with older members of the same sex, who reared and taught them.

In accordance with Mother Ann's advice, the pattern of Shaker days was established by work. Like their worldly neighbors, the Shakers were farm men and women whose principal business was providing food and clothing for the household. But the size of their Families permitted the Shakers an unusual opportunity for specialization and self-reliance. Shakers were blacksmiths, herbalists, broom makers, ministers, songwriters, business managers, physicians, school teachers, dairy workers, woodworkers, stone masons, bakers, shepherds, printers, shoemakers, cooks, and more. They produced much of what they needed at home and also made things to sell: boxes, brooms, packets of garden seeds and pharmaceutical herbs, and a wide range of other useful wares from wagons to candlesticks, depending on the community. Each Family had an Office, where members called Trustees conducted business transactions with the world outside. With good reason, the Shakers were respected for the quality of their products. "Do your work as if you had a thousand years to live, and as if you knew you would die tomorrow," Mother Ann had said. Productivity and excellence were expected and celebrated. A spiritual commitment to do things well combined with the temporal security that communalism provided allowed workers to pursue the highest levels of their crafts.

On the sabbath the Shakers gathered to worship in the Meetinghouse in order to achieve and express a sense of union through dance and song. Hundreds of Brothers and Sisters, wearing blue and white, stepped and bowed in rows on opposite sides of the room. Sometimes orderliness gave way to intensely private manifestations of the spirit by individuals, who spoke in tongues, communicated with angels, or whirled and leaped, transported by zeal. Shaker meetings were open to visitors from outside, who watched in wonder. To some, Shaker worship seemed the height of impropriety. But others glimpsed the hint of a powerful communion of spirit in the hypnotic rhythm of voices and feet.

The Shakers sacrificed much that the world outside held dear, including marriage, private property, and personal ambition. The promised reward was salvation hereafter, but there was clearly something appealing about Shaker life on earth as well. Simplicity, order, a strong sense of belonging—these were the qualities that drew and held converts. By 1831 the Shakers had witnessed a rise in membership for more than a half century. There seemed no reason to believe it would not continue. Those who built the dwelling here in that year saw it as an emblem of their founder's promise fulfilled. "The work is all well done," wrote the Elder in charge of construction. "There is none to excel it in this country. . . . As we have given in obedience to our good Mother Ann's words, so we expect to receive. Her precious words were these, 'Your hands to work and your hearts to God and a blessing will attend you.' This we have found true." It was beyond the imagination of the Sister who sat in her new room in the glory of the afternoon that the shining halls would ever be empty. The millennium, it seemed, had come.

The Shakers in this community and others grew in number during the following decade, but their energy was that of momentum, not creation. No new communities were established. Fewer converts came. Many children reared by the Shakers did not choose to remain as adults and sought their futures in the world that glittered outside. Members grew old and died; replacements did not come.

Before the Hancock dwelling house was twenty years old, the loss was felt in this Family. "On going into the wash room a few days ago, one of the Sisters who was to work there alone, mentioned to me what a lonesome feeling she had come across her that afternoon, and remarked that if all the folks were only here that had gone away in all these years, it had no need to be so, as she could then have help & company enough," wrote the Ministry Elder in 1848. Three years later, the community's South Family ceased to exist. Its buildings were closed, and the few remaining members moved into other areas of the village. It was a sad celebration of the twentieth anniversary of the splendid Church Family dwelling house.

Membership dwindled throughout the communities, and the Shaker sect weakened as Families closed, one by one. Properties were sold, and buildings fell into disrepair or were dismantled. In 1875 an entire community folded. Industries ceased, and fields gave way to saplings and grew into forest again. By the turn of the twentieth century, four more communities had closed, and others were approaching their end. By the First World War, only one Family remained of the original six in this community. The Church Family dwelling, nearing its ninetieth year, was home for a handful of aging members. There came a day—I don't know the month or year—when the last Sister who lived in this room left it for the last time. As in the days before its first inhabitancy in 1831, the room stood empty, but the silence this time was of conclusion, not anticipation.

Today, just two communities remain active, with fewer than a dozen members combined, in Maine and New Hampshire. Most of them came to the sect as children near the turn of the century. There are still some buildings where Shakers dwell, rooms warm and full with the business of life. We value the time we have spent with the Shakers who continue to live among us. But it has been those other rooms, the quiet empty places, that have drawn us in the making of this book.

Like exquisite shells, those buildings are empty now of living creatures but nonetheless marvelous to behold. Like shells they hold whispers of their past: just as we hear the sea in an empty shell, so we sense the presence of the Shakers in these quiet corners and luminous halls. In our different ways, Linda Butler and I have explored these realms of stillness and light.

That light-filled room where I go to write is an office now in a restored museum village. No Shaker has lived here for a quarter century and more. Age has traced its plaster with faint lines, like wrinkles in old skin, and dimmed its bright yellow and orange to gold and rust; but it wears its one hundred and fifty years with grace. The moment of late-afternoon radiance fades, as I know it will. A slant of light traces a familiar path on the floor as the earth turns toward the night and the room gathers the soft gray dusk.

JUNE SPRIGG
Pittsfield, Massachusetts
1984

INNER LIGHT

1 . SPIRAL STAIRS I

Pleasant Hill, Kentucky

2. CENTRE FAMILY DWELLING HOUSE

Pleasant Hill, Kentucky

3. MINISTRY SHOP HALLWAY

Sabbathday Lake, Maine

4. BONNET IN OVAL BOX

Hancock, Massachusetts

5 . CLOCK

New Lebanon, New York

6. MEETING ROOM

Sabbathday Lake, Maine

7. MEETING HOUSE FENCE I

Pleasant Hill, Kentucky

8. CHURCH FAMILY BUILDINGS

Sabbathday Lake, Maine

9. CLOAK POCKET

Hancock, Massachusetts

10. KITCHEN BOWLS
Hancock, Massachusetts

11. INFIRMARY CUPBOARD

Canterbury, New Hampshire

12. DWELLING HOUSE ATTIC

Canterbury, New Hampshire

13. SCARNE

Sabbathday Lake, Maine

14. GRAVESTONES

Alfred, Maine

15. MEETING HOUSE

Canterbury, New Hampshire

16. SHAKER GRAVEYARD

Harvard, Massachusetts

17. COLANDER AND SPOON

Pleasant Hill, Kentucky

18. MILK BUCKETS

Hancock, Massachusetts

19. SEED BOXES

Pleasant Hill, Kentucky

20. MEETING HOUSE FENCE II

Sabbathday Lake, Maine

21. WRITING DESK

Pleasant Hill, Kentucky

22. BROOMS

Hancock, Massachusetts

23. LAUNDRY ROOM

Hancock, Massachusetts

24. TABLEWARE

Hancock, Massachusetts

25 . SIEVES

Old Chatham, New York

26. WASHSTAND

Hancock, Massachusetts

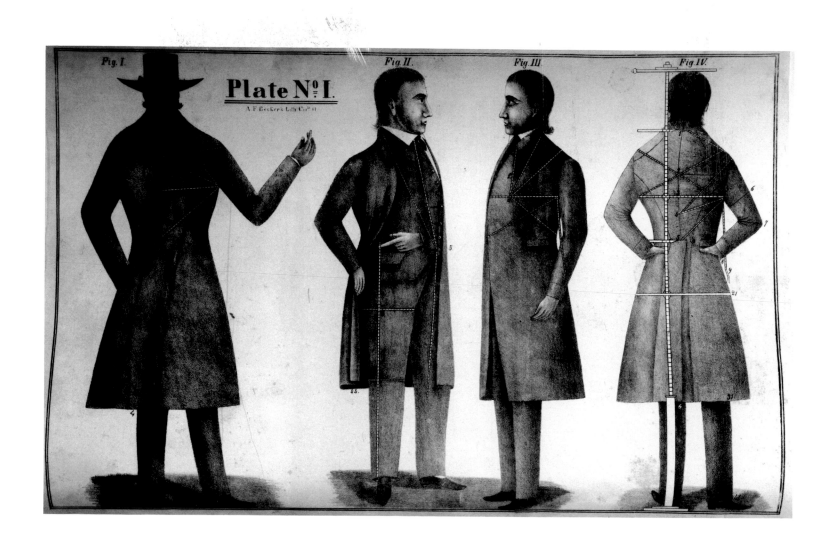

27. TAILOR'S DIAGRAM

Harvard, Massachusetts

28. DISTORTED PANES

Canterbury, New Hampshire

29. BASKETS

Sabbathday Lake, Maine

30. STOCKING FORMS

Canterbury, New Hampshire

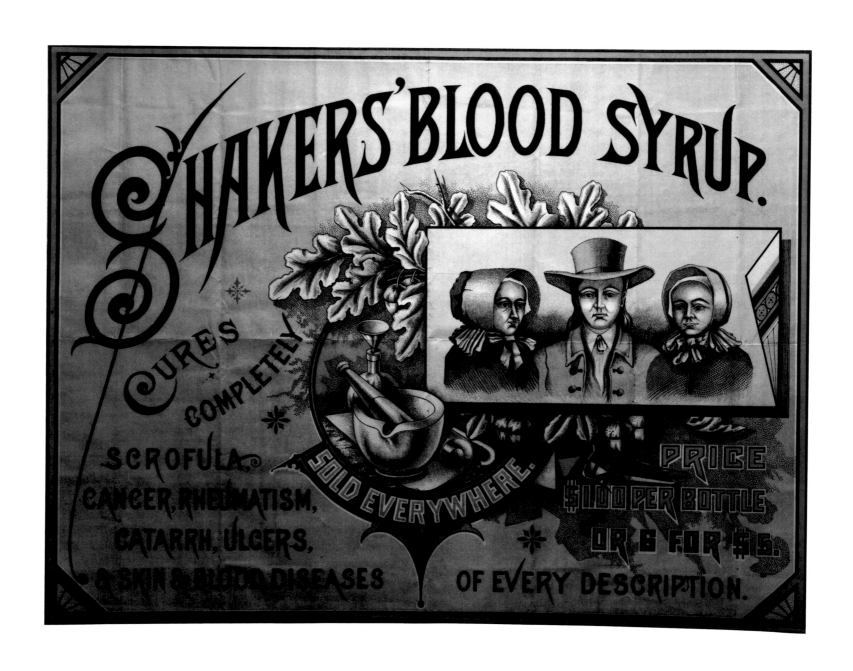

31. SHAKERS' BLOOD SYRUP

Old Chatham, New York

32. HAT MOLDS

Hancock, Massachusetts

33 . TINSMITH'S TOOLS
Pleasant Hill, Kentucky

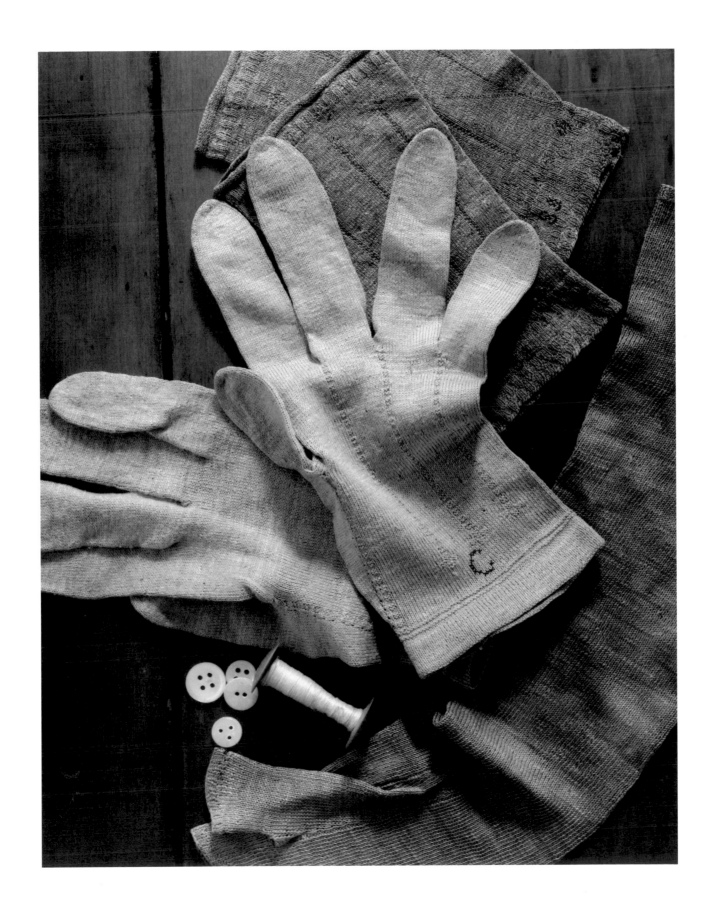

34. C'S GLOVES

Hancock, Massachusetts

February 1843.

bending & twisting, it looks beautiful, says Father,
we must all become fools for Christs sake.
remember that the young Brethren & Sisters need to
learn to be simple for themselves, & gain that mortifi-
cation which they need, in order to be able to help others
& this work is calculated to help them, as well as the
uncultivated Spirits.

    Brother Asa Brocklebank showered love upon
us, Shouted & leaped for joy:
    says Brother Asa, all the sufferings that have
been in this place, have not been for nothing, I
see this place Shine with the glory of God.
Deacon Nathan, Oliver Burt, Samuel Barrett, & James
Melvin & several others spoke, & showered their
love upon us, Shouted & leaped for joy, &c (this
was a very joyful & heavenly time.) we now
closed our visit with our heavenly Parents gave
them our thanks & love & bade them farewell.
    The Natives pressed in upon us, & begged a little
bit of privilege, we sung two or three of their songs,
hooped, hooted & rejoiced with them, & then dis-
missed, & found we had been in Meeting
two & ½ hours.

Thursday 9.
Meeting as usual. Read a Roll from Holy Mother
to the Youth. The Natives & other Spirits were admitted.
had lively exercise first — a new Company of the
Cherokee Tribe came; The chief of the tribe spoke, &c.
& then traveled. Many spoke & acted for the Natives.

Friday 10.
    We have communication from Harvard, thro' the
Company of Natives who went with the Ministry
there to stay a week, & have now returned. Some of
them prepare some Junky, Beer, cake, Strawberries,
&c & place upon our Supper table for us to partake
it was spoken of at the table & after we eat our native
food, we eat of the other &c. They brot a letterbag of
love from the Shiney Priests at Harvard. &c
    We had an Indian Meeting with the young, &
the aged had Union Meeting in the Chamber.

February 1843.

These Natives who had been to Harvard seemed quite
pleased to relate over their visit, &c, they Brot a Canoe
full of Love from the Brethren & Sisters, & from the
Natives there &c. told how much they had learn-
ed there &c how the Shiney foolks, took them in,
talked good to them & gave them great deal Love, &c.

Saturday 11.
We had a very good Meeting among ourselves; no
Inspiration. 1 hour long.

Sabbath 12.
Union Meeting in the A.M. & at 2 P.M. had a standing
Meeting in the dwelling house. Begun with the slow manner
two songs. then Marched two or three songs. then labored
in our rooms. Broke bands. had many simple gifts,
& a good Meeting, No Inspiration.
in the evening we have standing Meeting, & admit the
Spirits of different Nations; had a very singular
& strange Meeting. The spirits of many Nations were in,
Affricans, French, Spanish, Turks, Hotentots, &
Natives. had various exercises, strange gestures &
Speeches, &c, also many presents were given, such
as Tropical fruits, Barley Cakes, Strawburies, parch-
ed corn & &ying &c. after Meeting Elders
received Pine Apples, Grapes, , & some pipes to
smoke in from the French, & Turks, also some
Musical Instruments &c called the Flagulett.
Elders smoked & conversed some with them, &c the
French Sister gave a Basket of Oranges to be kept
in Ministry. &c.

Monday 13.
had standing Meeting, No Inspiration.

Thursday 16.
Meeting as usual. Admitted the Spirits
of Nations. Elders spoke considerable, to
bring into more order, & not have so much
confusion. Had a very good Meeting, Marched

36. MINISTRY'S RETIRING ROOM

Sabbathday Lake, Maine

37 . PARALLEL STAIRS I

Pleasant Hill, Kentucky

38. HAT AND BOX

Pleasant Hill, Kentucky

39. SKYLIT ATTIC

Pleasant Hill, Kentucky

40. RETIRING ROOM

Pleasant Hill, Kentucky

41. PARALLEL STAIRS II

South Union, Kentucky

42. WET STEPS

Sabbathday Lake, Maine

43 · CORN BREAD PANS

Pleasant Hill, Kentucky

44. STONE FLOOR

Hancock, Massachusetts

45 · BENT LIGHT

Pleasant Hill, Kentucky

46. DWELLING HOUSE DOOR

Pleasant Hill, Kentucky

47 . ORCHARD IN FOG

Sabbathday Lake, Maine

48. CHURCH FAMILY BUILDINGS

Hancock, Massachusetts

49. ROUND BARN INTERIOR

Hancock, Massachusetts

50. PEG SHADOWS

Canterbury, New Hampshire

51. SPIRAL STAIRS II

Pleasant Hill, Kentucky

5 2 . DWELLING HOUSE ARCH

Pleasant Hill, Kentucky

5 3 . SHOE LAST SHADOWS

Pleasant Hill, Kentucky

54 . DWELLING HOUSE HALLWAY

Hancock, Massachusetts

55. BONNET ON PEG

Hancock, Massachusetts

56. SONGBOOK

Pleasant Hill, Kentucky

57. CUPOLA

Pleasant Hill, Kentucky

I have found Fathers and Mothers, Brethren and Sisters in a strange land—real cincer faithful Christian travelars with whoom sincerely Loveing in the truth I feel willing to live and die—

Brother Solomon Butler (1774–1837)
Sabbathday Lake, Maine

58. EAST FAMILY BUILDINGS

Pleasant Hill, Kentucky

The Villages and Museums

The photographs in this book were taken in the following places:

THE DARROW SCHOOL
New Lebanon, New York

The New Lebanon Shaker community (1787–1947), on the New York–Massachusetts border, was the largest and most important Shaker settlement in the east. The second oldest settlement, it was also the home of the Shakers' supreme authority, the Parent Ministry. Rules and patterns established at the "Holy Mount" were obeyed in all other communities. By 1840 there were hundreds of buildings and about six hundred members.

The community suffered a disastrous fire in 1875 and thereafter slipped into decline. On a late afternoon in October 1904, Henry James found there "the strangest air of active, operative death ... the final hush of passions, desires, dangers. . . ."

Today, the surviving buildings have been converted to use by The Darrow School, a private secondary school; by individuals for residences; and by a group of Sufis for use as a communal home.

HANCOCK SHAKER VILLAGE
Pittsfield, Massachusetts

In 1783, Mother Ann Lee traveled through the Berkshires on a proselytizing mission. The Hancock Shaker community (1790–1960) gathered and grew just five miles from the settlement at New Lebanon, New York. By 1840, Hancock had nearly two hundred fifty members. Then as now, the centerpiece of the village was the Round Stone Barn (1826), which proved a grand attraction for neighboring farmers and sightseers.

The Hancock community was among the last three Shaker villages remaining occupied by Shakers when it closed in 1960. It passed directly into the hands of a nonprofit museum organization, which has since restored more than twenty buildings and brought traditional activities once more to workshops, gardens, and kitchen in the "City of Peace."

THE FRUITLANDS MUSEUMS
Harvard, Massachusetts

In 1781, Mother Ann Lee preached in the towns to the west of Boston. The Harvard Shaker community (1791–1918) grew within ten miles of a settlement at Shirley (1793–1909). The Shakers here were neighbors to Thoreau, Emerson, and Amos Bronson Alcott, the father of Louisa May Alcott, who established his own short-lived version of utopia, named Fruitlands, nearby. When Emerson visited the Shaker Elders at Harvard in 1845, he informed them that "too much interference" was his chief objection to their way of life.

Both communities were among the earliest to close. But the early twentieth-century efforts of a remarkable local woman, Clara Endicott Sears, resulted in the preservation of many artifacts at the Fruitlands Museums, the original home of Alcott's venture. The museum complex includes four major collections: the original Fruitlands farmhouse; an American Indian museum; a gallery of nineteenth-century American paintings; and the Shaker House (1794), which was moved to the site in 1920 from the Harvard community.

The Shirley community was converted for use as an industrial school and later for use as a state prison. Today the surviving buildings of the Harvard community are privately maintained as residences.

SHAKER VILLAGE
Canterbury, New Hampshire

Word of Ann Lee's activities reached New Hampshire in the early 1780s. Within a decade, two communities had gathered: at Enfield (1793–1923), near Hanover; and at Canterbury, near Concord, in 1792.

Set high in a rolling granite landscape, the Canterbury village attracted the attention of young Nathaniel Hawthorne, who admired the community's ethic—and its cider. He based two stories, *The Canterbury Pilgrim* and *The Shaker Bridal,* on his experience there. (Later, Hawthorne's enthusiasm palled. When he visited the Shakers at Hancock, Massachusetts, in 1851, his observations were not approving.)

The Canterbury community, noted for progressiveness in education and other matters, is one of two communities where Shakers continue to live. Today it is the home of the Central Ministry. In 1974, concerned for the future of their home, the remaining Sisters provided for the creation of a nonprofit museum organization to ensure the continuing preservation of their village and its lands. Visitors are welcome and may tour several buildings from late spring through early fall.

THE UNITED SOCIETY OF SHAKERS
Sabbathday Lake, Maine

Missionaries brought Ann Lee's message to Maine in the early 1780s, and two settlements eventually formed. A Shaker community at Alfred was formally gathered in 1793 and the Sabbathday Lake community, not far from Portland, in 1794. When the Alfred community closed in 1931, its remaining members joined the society at Sabbathday Lake. The buildings at Alfred are now home to the Brothers of Christian Instruction, a Catholic order.

The Sabbathday Lake community is one of two villages where Shakers continue to live. The Shakers here maintain several traditional activities, including sheep raising and herb processing. Several buildings are open seasonally for tours, and visitors may ask to join worship services on Sundays.

SHAKERTOWN AT PLEASANT HILL
Harrodsburg, Kentucky

On January 1, 1805, three Shaker Brethren from New York began a walk of a thousand miles to bring Ann Lee's message to what was then the American west in Kentucky and Ohio. Within a decade, four communities had been established. By 1826, two more societies had formed.

The Pleasant Hill Shaker community (1814–1910) was one of two Shaker settlements in Kentucky. It gathered and grew in the lush bluegrass region near Lexington. Although far from the central Shaker authority in New York, the Shakers here maintained remarkable similarity to their eastern Brethren and Sisters. They were superior farmers and also raised silkworms to produce fine silk.

In 1961, a half century after the community closed, a nonprofit museum organization began to plan for the restoration of the surviving buildings. Today, visitors may tour collections and buildings throughout the year. Some of the original structures have been converted to lodgings and an inn, so guests may stay on the grounds.

SHAKERTOWN
South Union, Kentucky

The South Union Shaker community (1807–1922) quickly grew to include almost three hundred and fifty members by 1830. While the Civil War caused problems for Shakers everywhere because the Brethren refused to serve in the military or engage in warfare, it was in Kentucky that the hardships were greatest. The South Union Shakers endured army encampments and survived into the twentieth century.

Fewer than ten of the community's approximately one hundred seventy-five buildings survive. They have been converted to use by St. Mark's Benedictine Monastery and by private owners for farming. In 1960, a nonprofit museum organization was founded to restore four buildings. Today, from spring through fall, visitors may tour the Centre Family Dwelling House, distinguished by the preservation of its original red and mustard-yellow paint on much of the interior woodwork.

THE SHAKER MUSEUM
Old Chatham, New York

While the Shaker Museum is not the site of an original Shaker community, it houses one of the largest and oldest assemblages of Shaker artifacts and an extensive library of Shaker records. This premier study collection is housed in ten buildings, originally the farm and home of John S. Williams, who began to collect in the 1930s and who founded the museum in 1950. Visitors may tour from late spring through fall.

Notes on the Photographs

1. SPIRAL STAIRS I
Trustees' Office (begun 1839, finished 1841)
Centre Family
Pleasant Hill, Kentucky

This spiral staircase is one of a pair that is unique in Shaker architecture. The cherry banister is made of forty-inch sections joined to form the curve.

Each Shaker Family had an Office, where members serving as Trustees conducted business affairs with the world outside.

2. CENTRE FAMILY DWELLING HOUSE
(begun 1824, finished 1834)
Pleasant Hill, Kentucky

The symmetry of the large communal limestone Dwelling House, curiously violated by the off-center cupola, exemplifies Shaker ideals of balance and order.

Double doors, a standard feature of Shaker domestic architecture, reflect the sect's beliefs in separation and equality of the sexes. Celibate Brethren and Sisters used separate doors and occupied separate sides of the building.

3. MINISTRY SHOP HALLWAY
Ministry Shop (built 1839, remodeled 1875)
Church Family
Sabbathday Lake, Maine

The windows over the door were designed to "borrow" light from a sunlit area and bring it into a darker part of the hall.

The two Elders and two Eldresses of the Maine Ministry used this building as a residence and workshop.

4. BONNET IN OVAL BOX
Hancock, Massachusetts

This box is made of maple and pine. Bonnets and oval boxes were among the wide variety of simple, useful objects made by the Shakers for themselves and for sale.

5. CLOCK
New Lebanon, New York

Brother Benjamin Youngs, Sr. (1736–1818), an early Shaker convert, made several clocks for the community at Watervliet, New York, including this tall clock from 1806. In later years Benjamin signed his work more inconspicuously, on the reverse of the dial, in accordance with Shaker beliefs, which emphasize community rather than self.

6. MEETING ROOM
Meeting House (1794)
Church Family
Sabbathday Lake, Maine

Shaker Meeting Houses were plain. Benches were movable, not fixed, so the Shakers could clear the floor for the distinctive dance worship that gave them their name. Visitors sat in built-in pews along the walls.

Shakers have gathered to worship in this room since 1794. Today, the service includes speaking and singing, but not dancing, which ceased to be part of Shaker worship practice by the early twentieth century.

7. MEETING HOUSE FENCE I
Church Family
Pleasant Hill, Kentucky

Snows of several inches are not uncommon in Kentucky, but heavy snows were more familiar to the Shakers in New England and New York.

8. CHURCH FAMILY BUILDINGS
Sabbathday Lake, Maine

The Shakers formally gathered here as a community in 1794. Today, it is one of two communities in which Shakers continue to live.

The buildings in this view date from the late eighteenth century through 1910. They include a Trustees' Office, Cart and Carriage Shed, Stable and Ox Barn, Garage, Spin House, Boys' Shop, and Herb House.

9. CLOAK POCKET
Hancock, Massachusetts

Shaker Sisters in several communities made fine woolen cloaks for themselves and for sale. This inside pocket shows the Shakers' attention to detail; the seams' raw edges are carefully pinked to prevent fraying.

10. KITCHEN BOWLS
Hancock, Massachusetts

Shaker Sisters took turns in the kitchen, preparing meals for communal Families of as many as one hundred members.

The bowls and rolling pin are unusually large—the bigger bowl is over two feet across.

11. INFIRMARY CUPBOARD
Infirmary (built 1811, remodeled 1849)
Church Family
Canterbury, New Hampshire

The medicine bottles remain as they were left early in this century. The cultivation of pharmaceutical herbs and the production of medicinal extracts were major Shaker industries.

12. DWELLING HOUSE ATTIC
Dwelling House (built 1793, remodeled 1837)
Church Family
Canterbury, New Hampshire

The Brethren and Sisters in this large Dwelling House were assigned drawers for storage of off-season clothing. There are over eighty drawers and seven walk-in closets. The wood is pine, stained yellow.

The advantages of built-in storage were order and cleanliness. There were no surfaces to catch dust underneath or on top.

13. SCARNE
Sabbathday Lake, Maine

The large spools on the scarne were wound with the warp threads for a loom. The spools kept the threads in order while a Sister tied the warp onto the loom.

14. GRAVESTONES
Alfred, Maine

In the twentieth century, individual markers in several communities were replaced with a single monument inscribed "Shakers"—a change that reduced the work of graveyard maintenance and underscored the communal nature of the sect.

15. MEETING HOUSE
(1792)
Church Family
Canterbury, New Hampshire

According to Shaker records, construction of this Meeting House proceeded in reverent silence—"scarcely a word was spoken . . . except a whisper."

The view is from the bell tower of the Church Family Dwelling House.

16. SHAKER GRAVEYARD
Harvard, Massachusetts

Shaker grave markers were very simple. The names and dates of the deceased were considered sufficient information. Some communities used initials only. These cast iron markers, made after 1873 to replace the original stones, are atypically ornate.

17. COLANDER AND SPOON
Pleasant Hill, Kentucky

The tin colander was used in cheesemaking. Whey dripped from the curds, which were wrapped in cheesecloth. Tinsmithing was one of the last surviving industries of the Pleasant Hill Shakers.

18. MILK BUCKETS
Hancock, Massachusetts

Shaker communities produced their own cheese and butter. The glass inserts in the sides of these tin buckets made it easy to measure the quantity of milk or cream they held.

19. SEED BOXES
Pleasant Hill, Kentucky

The Shakers were well known throughout the nineteenth century for marketing garden seeds. They were early in developing the small paper packet as standard packaging. Boxes with brightly colored labels displayed the seeds in stores.

20. MEETING HOUSE FENCE II
Church Family
Sabbathday Lake, Maine

Fences in Shaker villages had the practical function of separating pastures, roads, and fields from living areas. They also served the symbolic function of separating Shakers from the outside world.

21. WRITING DESK
Pleasant Hill, Kentucky

The leaders of the Shaker community used large desks for record keeping, daily accounts, and correspondence.

The hotel register in the foreground was a record kept by tenants in the twentieth century who converted Pleasant Hill's East Family Dwelling House into an inn, before its restoration as a museum building.

22. BROOMS
Hancock, Massachusetts

The Shakers have been credited with the development of the flat broom—a more efficient design than the traditional round bundle of broom corn. Mass production of brooms and an efficient distribution system brought considerable income to several communities.

23. LAUNDRY ROOM
(c. 1790–1800)
Church Family
Hancock, Massachusetts

> Sort your clothes and put every sort and kind together. . . . And whether you wash with soda or without it, have your clothes washed clean, boiled and rinsed well. This with a little blueing will make them look very well. . . . After the washing is finished, clean the tubs, pails and dippers. . . . Don't forget to be prudent of soap.
>
> *Eldress Cassandana Goodrich, 1841*

Shaker Sisters were responsible for washing clothes and bedding for Families of up to one hundred members.

To make laundry work easier, many communities developed efficient water systems, indoor drying lofts, and industrial-size washing machines.

24. TABLEWARE
Hancock, Massachusetts

> Never put on silver spoons for me nor tablecloths, but let your
> tables be clean enough to eat on without cloths; and if you do
> not know what to do with them, give them to the poor.
>
> *Mother Ann Lee (1736–1784)*

Following the teaching of their founder, the Shakers considered silver to
be an extravagance and used plain wooden- and bone-handled steel forks
and knives.

25. SIEVES
Old Chatham, New York

Sieves made of horse hair were useful for sifting flour and meal, paint
pigments, and dried powdered herbs.

26. WASHSTAND
Hancock, Massachusetts

This washstand, made at Hancock in about 1850, is typical of Shaker
furniture. Simple, functional, and carefully constructed, it is made of
pine and maple. The slight flare of the rim is an example of the subtle
virtuosity of Shaker master craftsmen.

The Shakers purchased plain white earthenware like this pitcher and
bowl.

27. TAILOR'S DIAGRAM
Harvard, Massachusetts

Shaker tailors used this diagram to measure individual Brethren for
"coats, vests, frocks, and trowsers." It is part of *The Tailor's Division System*,
published in 1849 by Elder Hervey L. Eades (1807–1892), of Union
Village, Ohio, and South Union, Kentucky.

Shaker clothing was simple, uniform, and well made but designed
without regard for fashion.

28. DISTORTED PANES
North Shop (1841)
Church Family
Canterbury, New Hampshire

The old glass panes in this window distort the view of the Laundry across
the road. The stairs lead to an attic in this workshop and storage
building.

29. BASKETS
Sabbathday Lake, Maine

The Shakers used baskets woven of ash splint to gather herbs, fruit, and
vegetables or to hold laundry. Some of these baskets remain in use by the
Shakers who live in this community.

30. STOCKING FORMS
Laundry (built 1795, remodeled through 1906)
Church Family
Canterbury, New Hampshire

Stockings knit of cotton, wool, or linen were dried on wooden forms to
keep them from shrinking or losing their shape.

31. SHAKERS' BLOOD SYRUP
Old Chatham, New York

The commercial success of the Shaker medicinal industry led to imitations.
"Shakers' Blood Syrup," which promised cures for cancer and other
maladies, was not a Shaker product but the offering of a company in
Canada.

32. HAT MOLDS
Hancock, Massachusetts

The wooden molds were used to shape Brethren's wide-brimmed hats. Men wore straw or palm leaf hats in summer and felt hats in winter.

33. TINSMITH'S TOOLS
Pleasant Hill, Kentucky

The compass, measuring stick, and enormous shears were used to make tinware.

34. C'S GLOVES
Hancock, Massachusetts

> The initials of a person's name, are sufficient mark to put upon any tools, or garment, for the purpose of distinction. Blue and white thread should generally be used for marking garments.
> *Millennial Laws, 1845*

These linen and woolen mitts and gloves, like all Shaker possessions, belonged to the community rather than to an individual.

For the sake of order, however, the Shakers deemed it proper to mark their garments with initials.

35. "THE CHURCH JOURNAL"
Harvard, Massachusetts

The Shakers were avid record keepers. This journal records the spiritual life of the Church Family at Shirley, Massachusetts, from 1843 through 1860. The entries range from "no inspiration" to vivid descriptions of visitations from the spirit world.

36. MINISTRY'S RETIRING ROOM
Meeting House (1794)
Church Family
Sabbathday Lake, Maine

This room on the third floor served as sleeping quarters for visiting Ministry Eldresses. The low door, with its original blue paint, provides access to storage space under the eaves.

37. PARALLEL STAIRS I
Dwelling House (begun 1824, finished 1834)
Centre Family
Pleasant Hill, Kentucky

Separate staircases for Sisters and Brethren were required in Shaker dwellings.

38. HAT AND BOX
Pleasant Hill, Kentucky

The hand-drawn design on the inside of the box is titled "On Times of All Nations." The minutes differ as well as the hours—perhaps evidence of a not-yet-standardized system of time zones.

39. SKYLIT ATTIC
Dwelling House (begun 1824, finished 1834)
Centre Family
Pleasant Hill, Kentucky

The Shakers commonly put windows or skylights in their attics for ventilation and to lessen the danger of fire from candles and lamps.

40. RETIRING ROOM
Dwelling House (begun 1824, finished 1834)
Centre Family
Pleasant Hill, Kentucky

> All are required to rise in the morning at the signal given for that purpose; and when any rise before the usual time they must not be noisy.

> All who sleep in a room must go to bed at the same time, and together, if not prevented by other duties.
>
> *Millennial Laws, 1845*

The communal, celibate Shakers shared bedrooms, which they called retiring rooms, with members of the same sex. Sleeping quarters were simply furnished with little more than a bed and a chair for each occupant. The tin ball at the foot of the bed was filled with an herbal mixture to repel insects.

41. PARALLEL STAIRS II
Dwelling House (begun 1822, finished 1833)
Centre Family
South Union, Kentucky

It was common practice for the carpenters of one community to help another community in major building projects; this explains some of the similarities among Shaker villages. Yet each Shaker Family made stylistic or proportional changes to create structures that suited their own needs.

42. WET STEPS
Meeting House (1794)
Church Family
Sabbathday Lake, Maine

Shaker Meeting Houses had separate entrances for Brethren and Sisters. The Shakers commonly added iron bootscrapers to steps so that those who entered could clean their shoes.

The building in the rear is the Ministry Shop (see Plate 3).

43. CORN BREAD PANS
Pleasant Hill, Kentucky

Shaker Sisters baked in large brick ovens that held dozens of pies or loaves of bread. These cast iron pans are heavy, but they retained heat well for baking.

44. STONE FLOOR
Tan House (1835)
Church Family
Hancock, Massachusetts

The Shakers sometimes laid stone floors in basements in preference to leaving bare earth. This building served a variety of purposes, including leather tanning, cider pressing, blacksmithing, and woodworking. The view is of the Ice House, built in 1894.

45. BENT LIGHT
Dwelling House (begun 1824, finished 1834)
Centre Family
Pleasant Hill, Kentucky

The members of the Centre Family gathered here for meetings and worship services. The arched transom over the door is typical of Shaker architecture in Kentucky.

In early morning and late afternoon, sunlight streams across the room and soars up the wall to curve back along the arched ceiling.

46. DWELLING HOUSE DOOR
Dwelling House (begun 1824, finished 1834)
Centre Family
Pleasant Hill, Kentucky

Mortise and tenon construction holds the door together. It was hand planed by the carpenters and painted a dark blue.

47. ORCHARD IN FOG
Sabbathday Lake, Maine

The Shakers raised and preserved a variety of fruits and vegetables for their own use and for sale. Orchards and gardens covered many acres in the nineteenth century. This orchard continues to produce a large crop of apples.

The structure is a water tank tower, built in 1903. The bell came from the Shaker community in Alfred, Maine.

48. CHURCH FAMILY BUILDINGS
Hancock, Massachusetts

Shakers lived in this community from 1790 until 1960. The view, from the attic of the Dwelling House, shows other buildings of the Church Family, including the Sisters' Shop in the foreground, the Tan House, the Round Stone Barn, and a 1910 barn in the background.

49. ROUND BARN INTERIOR
Round Stone Barn (built 1826, remodeled 1864)
Church Family
Hancock, Massachusetts

This large round barn is unique in Shaker architecture. Over fifty head of dairy cattle were housed on the main floor. Below was a manure pit, and above, a wagon level. Hay filled the center of the barn.

50. PEG SHADOWS
Dwelling House (begun 1795, remodeled through 1837)
Church Family
Canterbury, New Hampshire

Pegboards were a standard feature of Shaker interior architecture. This example is unusual because it follows the diagonal line of a dormer window in the attic. There are over two hundred pegs in this small space, which was used for off-season clothing storage.

51. SPIRAL STAIRS II
Trustees' Office (begun 1839, finished 1841)
Centre Family
Pleasant Hill, Kentucky

This staircase is one of a pair that spans three floors and culminates in a skylight (see Plate 1). It is thought that this design was inspired by the staircases in the Kentucky Capitol, completed in the early 1830s.

52. DWELLING HOUSE ARCH
Dwelling House (begun 1824, finished 1834)
Centre Family
Pleasant Hill, Kentucky

A pair of arches, one for men and one for women, is located at the entrance to the Meeting Room (see Plate 45).

Chairs not in use were hung on the pegboard to make cleaning and movement in the rooms easier.

53. SHOE LAST SHADOWS
Pleasant Hill, Kentucky

These wooden forms were used to make shoes. To attach the sole, the shoemaker pounded small wooden pegs through the layers of leather. Holes are visible along these lines in the shoe lasts.

54. DWELLING HOUSE HALLWAY
Dwelling House (begun 1830, finished 1831)
Church Family
Hancock, Massachusetts

Wide halls separated the rooms where Brethren and Sisters slept. One Shaker likened his celibate, communal sect to "monks and nuns, without the bolts and bars."

55 . BONNET ON PEG
Hancock, Massachusetts

Shaker Sisters covered their heads with palm leaf bonnets when they went outdoors. Inside, they wore white caps. The Kentucky Shakers produced much of the silk used to make the iridescent capes and ties.

56 . SONGBOOK
(1845)
Pleasant Hill, Kentucky

The Shakers composed many thousands of sacred songs, which they regarded as divinely inspired. Perhaps the most familiar of these "gift songs" is "Simple Gifts," which Aaron Copland used as a theme in *Appalachian Spring.* Until the late nineteenth century, the Shakers rejected harmony and instrumental accompaniment as unnecessary embellishment. Shaker musicians developed their own system of notation in the 1840s, which continued in use for several decades.

57 . CUPOLA
Dwelling House (begun 1824, finished 1834)
Centre Family
Pleasant Hill, Kentucky

This narrow cupola is perched atop the Centre Family Dwelling House (see Plate 2). It opens onto a walk on the roof which affords a fine overview of the Pleasant Hill acreage.

58 . EAST FAMILY BUILDINGS
Pleasant Hill, Kentucky

Brethren and Sisters of the East Family ate, slept, and worshipped in the large brick Dwelling House (1817) near the center of the photograph. Surrounding workshops include the Wash House and the Brethren's Shop. The building at the far right is the Trustees' Office.

The view is from the Centre Family Dwelling House.

Acknowledgments

This project gathered its energy from the people in Kentucky and New England who have lived or worked in the Shaker villages. A great many individuals—too many to list separately—contributed to the work. They guided me to the spaces and objects they thought I should see, challenging me to put on film what they had grown to love. Without this inspiration and encouragement, I could not have created these images.

I am particularly indebted to Ed Nickels, curator at Pleasant Hill, Kentucky, who opened the collection of Pleasant Hill to me and became my most trusted critic. I am also grateful to Faith Andrews, the early Shaker collector, whose knowledge of the Shaker spirit inspired several of the images; her delight with the photographs was tempered with a Shaker-like insistence on perfection.

The Shakers themselves contributed immeasurably to my understanding of their faith. At Canterbury, New Hampshire, on cold winter evenings, the Eldresses' thoughtful recollections would fill the village with the Shakers they had known. At Sabbathday Lake, Maine, the active study, worship, and work of the community there inspired a new insight into the early Shakers' communal life.

The staff at the two largest Shaker village-museums were particularly generous. Jim Thomas, president of Pleasant Hill, Kentucky, and Jane Brown, director of public relations, supported the project from its germination through its completion, setting the tone that allowed me to work so freely at Pleasant Hill. I am grateful to Jerry Grant, director of Hancock Shaker Village, Massachusetts, who guided me to the treasures of Hancock, and to Beverly Hamilton, assistant to the director, who patiently directed my use of fabrics and utensils that were in storage.

At each of the museums, the directors and staff made special arrangements for me to work with their delicate collections, often opening areas of their villages that were closed to the public. I would like to thank Richard Kathmann, director of Canterbury Shaker Village, Canterbury, New Hampshire; Jerral Miles, Headmaster of Darrow School, New Lebanon, New York; Julia Neal, former co-director of Shakertown at South Union, Kentucky; Richard Reed, director of the Fruitlands Museums of Harvard, Massachusetts; and Viki Sand, director of the Shaker Museum at Old Chatham, New York.

I appreciated the contribution of William Hennessey, director of the University of Kentucky Art Museum in Lexington, Kentucky, whose commitment to exhibit the photographs and continued support have given momentum to the project. Special thanks to my artist friends Carolyn Hisel, Ann Stewart Anderson, Barbara McCord, and Jonathan Greene, whose critiques helped to shape the direction of my work; and to Jean Schreier, Jan Graves, Susan Waters, and Teresa Watson, whose encouragement helped to sustain my energy.

I am especially grateful to Alice Quinn and Victoria Wilson, my editors at Knopf, who believed in the book and patiently directed its development, and to June Sprigg who created a lyrical text that is in such harmony with the photographs. I would also like to thank Dorothy Schmiderer, whose design synthesized the text and photos into a coherent whole, and Ellen McNeilly, whose experienced eye guided the production of the book.

Finally, I wish to thank my husband, Steven Nissen, whose loving support and confidence have given me much strength.

LINDA BUTLER

For help with the captions and text, I am indebted to Linda Butler, Alice Quinn, Ed Nickels, Priscilla Brewer, and Jerry Grant. Above all, love and thanks to Dick Davis, whose patient reading and thoughtful comments helped make the whole a better book.

JUNE SPRIGG

A NOTE ON THE TYPE

The text of this book was set in Centaur, the only type face designed by Bruce Rogers, the well-known American book designer. A celebrated penman, Rogers based his design on the roman face cut by Nicolas Jensen in 1470 for his Eusebius. Jensen's roman surpassed all of its forerunners and even today, in modern recuttings, is one of the most popular and attractive of all type faces.

The italic used to accompany Centaur is Arrighi designed by Frederic Warde, also an American, and based on a Chancery face used by Ludovico degli Arrighi in 1524.

A NOTE ON THE PRINTS

The negatives for these photographs were made with an 8 × 10 Deardorff camera using Ilford HP5 film. The originals were printed on Portriga Rapid paper and toned in selenium. Exposure times ranged from one-thirtieth of a second to forty-five minutes, averaging about three minutes.

Composed by Superior Type, Champaign, Illinois
Printed by Gardner/Fulmer Lithograph, Buena Park, California
Bound by A. Horowitz and Sons, Fairfield, New Jersey
Designed by Dorothy Schmiderer